MUSCULAR AND SKELETAL SYSTEMS

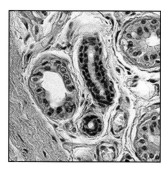
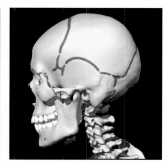

by Steve Parker

NEW
FOREST
PRESS

How to use this book

This book is your guide to yourself—an atlas of the human body. Follow the main text for an informative overview of a particular area of the body or use the boxes to jump to a specific area of interest. Finally, try some of the suggested activities and experiments to discover more about yourself!

Body Locator

Highlighted areas on the body locator help you learn your body's geography by indicating the area of the body organs or systems discussed on those pages.

Instant Info

Get instant, snappy facts that summarize the topic in just a few sentences. Discover which muscle is strongest, which bone is longest, and much more.

Health Watch

Read about illness and disease related to the relevant area of the body. For example, in the section about skin, learn what Sun damage can do to our cells and how we can protect ourselves.

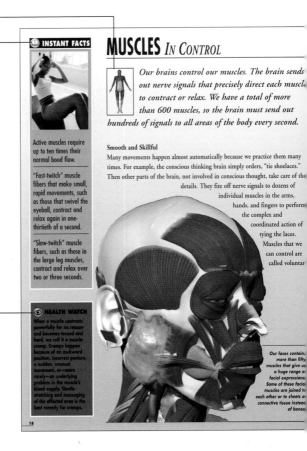

INSTANT FACTS

Active muscles require up to ten times their normal blood flow.

"Fast-twitch" muscle fibers that make small, rapid movements, such as those that swivel the eyeball, contract and relax again in one-thirtieth of a second.

"Slow-twitch" muscle fibers, such as those in the large leg muscles, contract and relax over two or three seconds.

HEALTH WATCH

When a muscle contracts powerfully for no reason and becomes tensed and hard, we call it a muscle cramp. Cramps happen because of an awkward position, incorrect posture, a sudden, unusual movement, or—more rarely—an underlying problem in the muscle's blood supply. Gentle stretching and massaging of the affected area is the best remedy for cramps.

MUSCLES In Control

Our brains control our muscles. The brain sends out nerve signals that precisely direct each muscle to contract or relax. We have a total of more than 600 muscles, so the brain must send out hundreds of signals to all areas of the body every second.

Smooth and Skillful

Many movements happen almost automatically because we practice them many times. For example, the conscious thinking brain simply orders, "tie shoelaces." Then other parts of the brain, not involved in conscious thought, take care of the details. They fire off nerve signals to dozens of individual muscles in the arms, hands, and fingers to perform the complex and coordinated action of tying the laces. Muscles that we can control are called voluntar

Our faces contain more than fifty muscles that give us a huge range of facial expressions. Some of these facial muscles are joined to each other or to sheets of connective tissue instead of bones.

Try It Yourself

Try these suggested activities to learn more. No special equipment is required—just your own body!

> **Metric Conversion Table
> on page 31**

In Focus

View stunning macroimagery and images of an anatomically correct digital model of body parts.

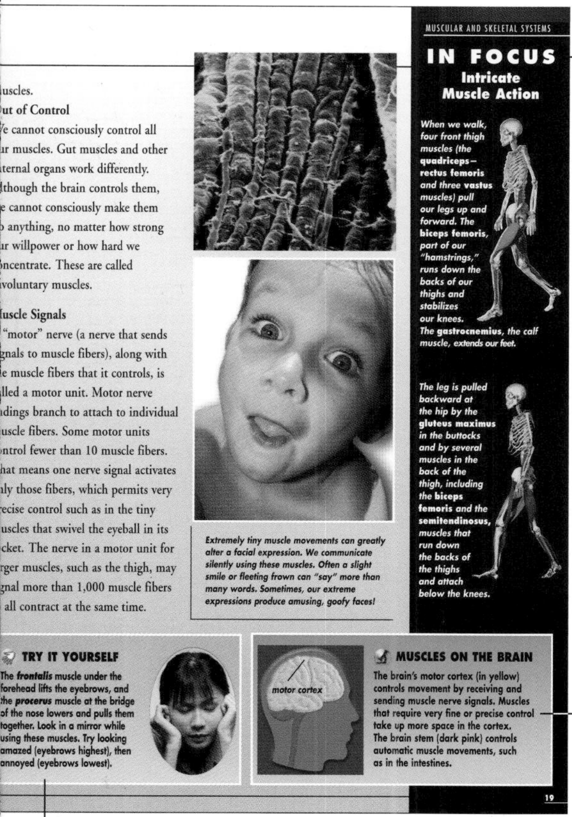

The following is text visible from an adjacent page reproduced within the "In Focus" example:

...uscles.

...ut of Control

...e cannot consciously control all ...ur muscles. Gut muscles and other ...ternal organs work differently. ...lthough the brain controls them, ...e cannot consciously make them ...o anything, no matter how strong ...ur willpower or how hard we ...oncentrate. These are called ...voluntary muscles.

...uscle Signals

...e "motor" nerve (a nerve that sends ...gnals to muscle fibers), along with ...e muscle fibers that it controls, is ...lled a motor unit. Motor nerve ...dings branch to attach to individual ...uscle fibers. Some motor units ...ntrol fewer than 10 muscle fibers. ...hat means one nerve signal activates ...ly those fibers, which permits very ...recise control such as in the tiny ...uscles that swivel the eyeball in its ...cket. The nerve in a motor unit for ...rger muscles, such as the thigh, may ...gnal more than 1,000 muscle fibers ...all contract at the same time.

MUSCULAR AND SKELETAL SYSTEMS

IN FOCUS
Intricate Muscle Action

When we walk, four front thigh muscles (the **quadriceps**— **rectus femoris** and three **vastus** muscles) pull our legs up and forward. The **biceps femoris,** part of our "hamstrings," runs down the backs of our thighs and stabilizes our knees. The **gastrocnemius,** the calf muscle, extends our feet.

The leg is pulled backward at the hip by the **gluteus maximus** in the buttocks and by several muscles in the back of the thigh, including the **biceps femoris** and the **semitendinosus,** muscles that run down the backs of the thighs and attach below the knees.

Extremely tiny muscle movements can greatly alter a facial expression. We communicate silently using these muscles. Often a slight smile or fleeting frown can "say" more than many words. Sometimes, our extreme expressions produce amusing, goofy faces!

TRY IT YOURSELF
The **frontalis** muscle under the forehead lifts the eyebrows, and the **procerus** muscle at the bridge of the nose lowers and pulls them together. Look in a mirror while using these muscles. Try looking amazed (eyebrows highest), then annoyed (eyebrows lowest).

MUSCLES ON THE BRAIN
motor cortex
The brain's motor cortex (in yellow) controls movement by receiving and sending muscle nerve signals. Muscles that require very fine or precise control take up more space in the cortex. The brain stem (dark pink) controls automatic muscle movements, such as in the intestines.

19

 ## *Diagrams*

Watch for in-depth scientific diagrams and explanations that focus on the details of a body part.

CONTENTS

Introduction

Welcome to a journey that will take you from the outermost surface of the body to its center. We begin with skin, the largest organ of your body, and one with many uses apart from its function as a protective cover. From there, we'll travel under your skin to expose the hundreds of muscles that allow for an endless variety of movements, from blinking to yawning. Our journey then reaches the body's innermost framework—the skeleton. Bones form the hardest, toughest parts of our bodies and last longest after death.

Outside to Inside

Body parts that work together to carry out one major purpose or function are known as a body system. Skin, hair, and nails make up the integumentary system. Just under them, another main body system, the muscles, create movement. This motion ranges from small movements of body parts, like the split-second blink of an eye or snap of the fingers, to full-body movements such as walking, running, or swimming.

The Inner Framework

Muscles cannot work alone. Most muscles are attached to bones and pull on them to create movement. Bones make up the skeletal system at the body's core. Its chief task is to provide a strong inner framework to support and protect the many softer parts such as the lungs, brain, and blood vessels. Since muscles and bones work together so closely, they are often regarded as one system—the musculoskeletal system.

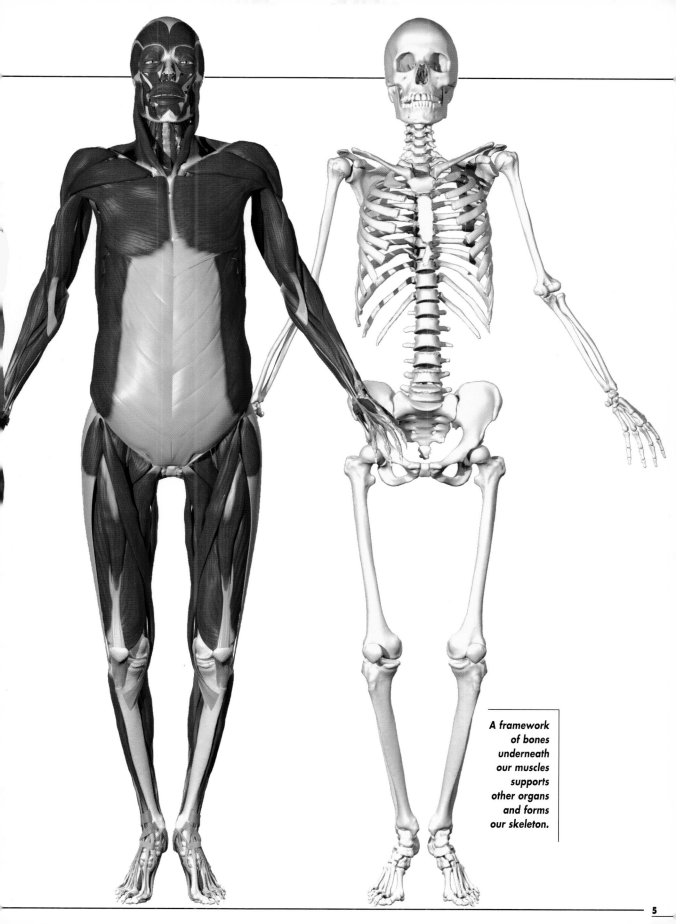

A framework
of bones
underneath
our muscles
supports
other organs
and forms
our skeleton.

SKIN *All Wrapped Up*

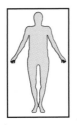

Your skin is far more than a simple covering that guards the body and provides protection from nicks and cuts. It also has a range of features and functions that warm you when it's cold, cool you when it's hot, and help you feel the world around you.

Skin is an adaptable shield that we constantly rub away. At the same time, this "living overcoat" renews itself continuously to maintain its thickness and protect the body. Our skin helps contain body fluids, minerals, nutrients, and other substances. It is a waterproof covering that keeps water from invading our internal organs when we laze in the bathtub or go swimming.

Self-Repairing Germ Barrier

Skin prevents harmful microbes (germs) from invading the internal systems. Damaged or wounded skin repairs itself to hold fluids in and keep germs out. Skin also forms a

HEALTH WATCH

Most people have a few marks and spots, such as moles and freckles—which are usually harmless—on their skin. If these areas change in some way, seek medical advice promptly. Watch for itchiness, bleeding, changes in color or size, or a sore that won't heal. Rarely, these changes indicate a malignant (cancerous) growth. Skin cancers are treated most successfully in their earliest stages.

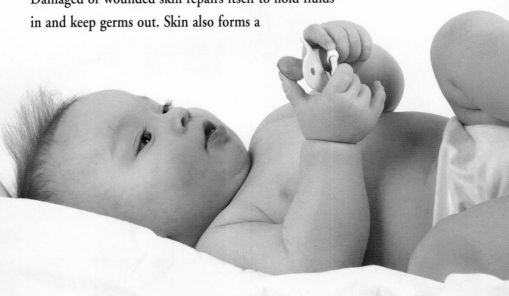

A subcutaneous (under the skin) layer of fat gives babies extra "padding" and protection. This layer gradually reduces in thickness with age. The skin itself also becomes thinner and more fragile. Older skin cuts more easily and takes longer to heal.

barrier that protects the delicate, moist internal organs from drying out as well as from other harm caused by solar (the Sun's) radiation. A tanned skin color indicates skin damaged by the Sun's ultraviolet (UV) wavelengths.

Hot and Cold

Our skin plays a vital role in keeping the body's temperature within narrow limits. If the body is too hot, our skin reddens and sweats to encourage heat loss. When the body is chilled, our skin becomes pale and its tiny hairs stand on end as "goose bumps" to conserve warmth. Skin also provides one of the body's five main senses: touch.

Our skin tells us not only if something is touching us, but also if that object is hard or soft, hot or cold. It also tells us if something is painful so we can protect ourselves against further harm.

Human skin is rarely more than one-fifth of an inch thick, except perhaps on the soles of the feet. An elephant's skin is ten times thicker, at two inches, and in total can weigh as much as four adults.

Skin begins life as soft and smooth as a baby's bottom. It gradually loses its softness and elasticity with age, forming ridges and wrinkles around curves, joints, and other areas where it is regularly stretched.

🖐 Try it Yourself

Gently pinch a fold of skin on the back of your hand between thumb and forefinger. Note the fold's thickness. Your skin itself is about half as thick. Try this on various body areas. Discover where on the body the skin is so strongly attached to the underlying parts that it cannot be lifted in a fold.

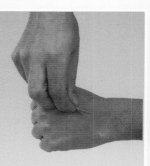

IN FOCUS
Your Skin Up Close

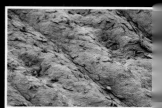

Magnified thousands of times, the skin's surface resembles the forbidding landscape of a far-off planet.

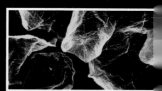

These loose, microscopic flakes form clumps of dead skin cells that absorb wear and impact. They fall away when their task is done.

🌐 The Rule of Nines

Burned skin is very painful. Serious burns cause fluid loss, risk of infection, and even death. Medical personnel use the "rule of nines" to describe the extent of the damage. If the burn damage exceeds 9 percent of the body, emergency care is urgent.

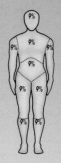

SKIN UNDER THE SURFACE

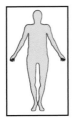

Every month, there's a "new you"! The entire outer surface of your skin—the epidermis—is replaced every four weeks. The main task of the waterproof epidermis is protection. Underneath that is the dermis, which is a much much more delicate and sensitive layer. You can feel the dermis when you accidentally scrape off the epidermis to expose the dermis. Ouch—that stings!

Multiply and Die!

At the base of the epidermis, millions of microscopic cells multiply rapidly, producing billions of cells every hour. These cells migrate upward as the constant multiplying produces even more cells beneath. As the epidermal cells rise to the surface, they fill with a tough substance, a protein called keratin, and flatten out. Once the epidermal cells reach the surface of your skin, they fall off. You lose skin cells everywhere you go!

sebaceous gland

sweat pore

sweat gland

epidermis

dermis

hair follicle

⚒ UNDER THE SKIN

Epidermis, dermis, and subcutaneous fat layers, as well as collagen and elastin fibers, appear throughout the body, but the thickness of the epidermis and dermis varies greatly. In most areas, the epidermis is ten times thinner than the dermis. In skin thickened by rubbing, such as on the sole of the foot or on the palm of the hand, the two layers are almost equal.

Under Your Skin

The dermis is fixed to the base of the epidermis. This busy layer is crammed full of tiny blood vessels and nerve endings that give us the sense of touch. The tiniest of the blood vessels are called capillaries. They bring nutrients and oxygen to the skin so that it can keep replacing itself. Roots of hairs and the coiled microtubes of sweat glands also begin at the bottom of the dermis. Sweat glands pierce the epidermis above to open at the surface. Connective-tissue fibers called collagen and elastin hold the layers together. Collagen gives skin its durable strength, while elastin allows skin to stretch and spring back as the body moves.

"Skin Deep"

Cells called melanocytes are scattered through the base layer of the epidermis. Melanocytes make tiny grains of a dark substance, a pigment called melanin. These grains pass into the epidermal cells, giving them color. All humans have the same number of melanocyte cells in their skin. Our genes control the amounts of melanin produced by our skin—which determines our skin color.

Melanin, a pigment produced by cells called melanocytes, gives our skin its color. When exposed to the Sun's UV rays, melanocytes become more active, making the epidermis darker—and we tan. Melanin pigment shields the underlying layers from more UV harm.

blood
vessels

subcutaneous
fat layer

collagen and
elastin fibers

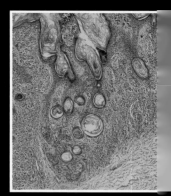
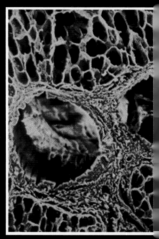
TRY IT YOURSELF

Sweating helps us grip. Pick up a small item like a paperclip. Then thoroughly wash and dry your hands and do it again. Now that you've removed the thin film of sweat, it's harder to grip and hold such tiny items.

A person with fair or blonde hair has the most individual hairs: about 130,000.

This number is lower for other colors—about 110,000 for brown, 100,000 for black, and 90,000 for red or ginger-colored hair.

A scalp hair lasts for up to five years, an eyebrow or eyelash hair for only ten weeks.

Head hairs lengthen by about a tenth of an inch each week, with fine, fair hair growing slightly slower than thick, dark hair.

👁 HEALTH WATCH

Detectives like hair! They can use it to help solve crimes because hair takes up traces of poisons, such as mercury and arsenic, passing through the body. Also, like skin, hair indicates general health. Hair that grows slowly and is thin and fragile may suggest a poor diet or generalized illness.

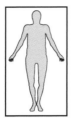

Most humans have more individual hairs (about 20 million) than a gorilla or a chimpanzee. The reason we look much less hairy is that our body hair is much shorter and thinner than ape hair. Early humans probably used their hair to help keep warm, but we mostly trim, style, color, or remove our hair.

The Life of a Hair

A hair does not live forever. We lose about 100 old hairs daily, while 100 new ones appear in different locations on the scalp. The only living part of hair is its base, or root, nestled inside a tiny pit in the skin called a hair follicle. Cells in the follicle multiply, fill with hard keratin, attach to the root as they glue themselves together into a rod shape, and rapidly die. This pushes the rest of the hair, called the shaft, gradually upward. Scalp and body hair grow at different rates before falling out. Each follicle rests for up to six months before sprouting a new hair, and the process begins again.

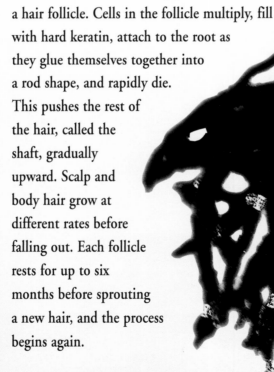

For some people, hair is a self-renewing fashion accessory that is colored and styled. Hair also has other uses. It offers protection against cold, heat, and UV rays. Sometimes, it's thick enough to cushion the head.

While apes such as orangutans have fewer individual hairs than humans, their body hairs are much longer and thicker. The long hair helps rainwater run off the ape's body in its tropical rain forest home.

Sliding Fingernails and Toenails

A fingernail or toenail grows from a root at the base of the nail. The nail lengthens as it slides slowly along its underlayer (the nail bed) toward its outer edge. Like hair and the epidermal skin layer, nails are made of the hard protein keratin. A fingernail forms a firm support to prevent the soft, fleshy fingertip from flexing too much. This allows us to press and pick up small objects and gauge the finger's pushing force. Try to scratch an itch without your fingernails. Toenails help in our balance as we feel the pushing pressure of our toes on the ground.

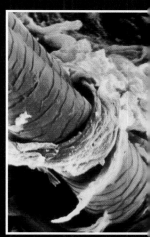

A hair is a scaly-looking cylinder of flattened, keratin-filled cells wrapped around an inner rod of longer cells.

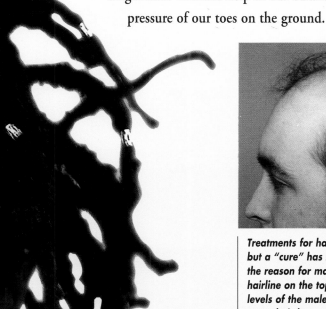

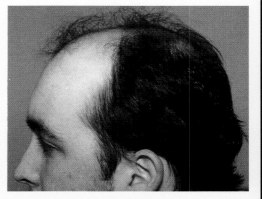

Treatments for hair loss are announced regularly, but a "cure" has still not been found. Part of the reason for male-pattern baldness (receding hairline on the top of the head) is genetic. Raised levels of the male hormone testosterone also cause hair loss.

By the time a hair shaft is tall enough to emerge from its follicle, it is completely dead.

🐾 TRY IT YOURSELF

Hair is amazingly strong, with a tensile (pulling) strength greater than steel wire of the same thickness. Try to break a long scalp hair. Compare its strength to cotton thread, which is about 100 times thicker—which do you think is stronger?

✍ HAIR FOLLICLES

A hair follicle is a pit in the epidermis that reaches into the dermis. Two important structures are associated with the follicle. One is the sebaceous gland. It makes the natural oils and waxes that keep our skin supple and water-repellent. The other is a tiny muscle, the *arrector pili* (*erector papilla*), which pulls the hair upright (see pages 12–13).

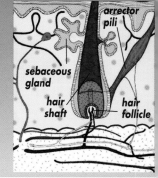

arrector pili

sebaceous gland

hair shaft

hair follicle

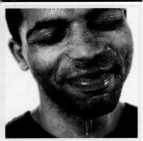
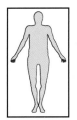

Overall, our skin has about three million sweat glands.

If you straightened and joined all the tiny sweat glands, they would stretch about 31 miles!

In normal conditions, our bodies produce just over one and a half cups of sweat daily.

An active body in hot conditions can lose more than half a gallon of sweat in one day.

HEALTH WATCH

Skin can ruin a vacation! Overexposure to ultraviolet rays causes sunburn. The skin turns red, swells, and blisters. If the temperature gets too hot for our skin to keep our body cool, our body temperature rises, and we get heatstroke. This causes confusion, cramps, and collapse. When the body gets too cold, we get hypothermia. Symptoms include intense shivering, pale skin color, and collapse.

SKIN *HOT AND COLD*

One of skin's most important tasks is regulating body temperature. Our skin can change from a warmth-retaining "overcoat" to a heat-producing "radiator" in just a few minutes. Our bodies work best at a constant temperature of 98.6° Fahrenheit (37° Celsius).

Cool It

When our body temperature climbs above normal, our skin helps us cool down several different ways. Nerve signals from the brain change the size of small blood vessels carrying blood to the skin's surface. When we are hot, the vessels widen, sending more blood through the skin, making it reddened or flushed. This helps rid the body of excess heat. When we are hot, we also release more water, called sweat (perspiration), from tiny glands in the skin. As this water dries, it draws heat away from the body. Finally, the tiny muscles that control the position of skin hairs spring into action to help us cool down. These hair muscles relax, making skin hair flatten—which helps body heat escape. Behavioral reactions kick in, too. We may seek shade, remove clothing, or fan ourselves.

Sweat is about 97 percent water, with dissolved salts and minerals such as sodium and potassium. As these are lost in sweat, they must be replaced to maintain the correct body-fluid balance. This is why some sports drinks contain more than just water.

We lose from 30 to 70 percent of our body heat from the head, face, and neck. A hat, hood, scarf, long hair, and—for men—a mustache and beard all help insulate the body in extra-cold conditions.

IN FOCUS
Sweating

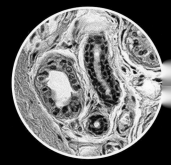

Sweat glands are curly tubes in the skin, here cut crossways. The sweat pore passes through the dermis and epidermis to open onto the skin's surface. Sweat glands on fingertips open along the skin ridges. Ink or powder sticks to this film of sweat to outline the ridge pattern in a fingerprint.

Heavier sweat appears during exercise or hot weather or when we feel nervous and worried. This microscope picture shows sweat droplets lying on the skin's surface. Glands in tiny holes, or pores, in the skin produce the salty, watery liquid called sweat.

Warming Up

Our skin automatically reacts if we get too cold. As body temperature drops, blood vessels narrow. Less blood flows to the skin, reducing heat loss from skin to air. Sweat glands release less sweat. Tiny muscles attached to each hair pucker the skin into small mounds that we call "goose bumps" or "goose pimples." These muscles also pull each hair upright, trapping an air layer near the skin to insulate the body and conserve heat. The larger body muscles also shiver and shake to generate warmth.

TRY IT YOURSELF

Put a clear plastic bag over your hand for a few minutes, tied loosely at the wrist. Watch as tiny water drops form inside the bag as sweat (perspiration) evaporates from your skin and condenses on the plastic. Your skin constantly releases a small amount of sweat, even if you stay still.

GOOSE BUMPS

A tiny muscle is attached to every hair in the skin. When we feel cold, worried, or frightened, the muscle pulls on the hair, tilting it upright. The muscle also heaps the skin around the hair into a tiny "hill" called a goose bump.

Most people have about 640 muscles.

Muscles shrink, or atrophy, from disuse.

Depending on the amount of other body tissues (especially fat), the muscular system makes up about 45 percent of an adult male body and about 35 percent of an adult female body.

The biggest single muscle is the gluteus maximus in the buttock. It pulls the thigh back at the hip while moving forward.

The stapedius, the smallest muscle, is thinner than a cotton thread and is found deep in the inner ear.

MUSCLES *MANY MUSCLES*

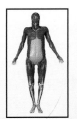

Working out in the gym, lifting weights, and "pumping iron" can't make your body develop more muscles. It can only make your muscles larger. Each individual muscle is made of very thin muscle fibers that can be enlarged through exercise.

Making Movements

The muscular system is by far the body's heaviest and bulkiest system, forming roughly two-fifths of an adult's weight. All of the body's hundreds of muscles move only one way—they contract, or get shorter. These contractions range greatly in force and speed, from lifting a heavy weight to the twitching of a finger.

Size and Shape

The body has muscles of almost every shape. Arm and leg muscles are the "typical" spindle-like shape—long and slim but wider and fleshy in the middle (the muscle's body, or belly). Some shoulder and hip muscles are triangular or rectangular, and others are branched like the letters V, Y, or W. Strap-shaped muscles run along the spine, while sheetlike muscles cover the front of the lower body. Most muscles attach to bones at each end. Others attach to other muscles or to sheets of tough, strong connective tissue.

frontalis

masseter

deltoid

pectoralis

biceps brachii

digital flexors

rectus abdominis

sartorius

rectus femoris

vastus lateralis

peroneus longus

soleus

MUSCLES

This view just under the skin shows the outermost, or superficial, muscles. Each of the body's hundreds of muscles has a name. Every part of every major muscle also has a name. Some muscles branch into two or more parts, called heads, that link to the same bones or to different bones. It's a very complicated arrangement that helps us move in amazing ways!

Humans and lions have almost exactly the same number of muscles. Many of the lion's muscles are proportionally larger and more powerful than a human's so that well over half of the big cat's bulk is muscle tissue.

IN FOCUS
Taking the Strain

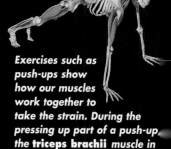

Exercises such as push-ups show how our muscles work together to take the strain. During the pressing up part of a push-up, the **triceps brachii** muscle in the back of the upper arm takes much of the pressure.

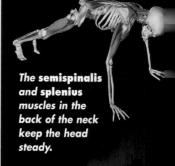

The **semispinalis** and **splenius** muscles in the back of the neck keep the head steady.

Pull or Push?

An individual muscle pulls by contracting (shortening) from its resting length. No muscle can forcefully lengthen, or push. This is one of the reasons that the muscular system is so complex. If one muscle pulls a body part one way, it cannot push it back again. Another muscle must pull the body part the opposite way. Muscles are usually arranged in opposing, or antagonistic, pairs and pull in opposite directions.

occipitalis

trapezius

deltoid

triceps brachii

digital extensors

latissimus dorsi

gluteus maximus

semitendinosus

biceps femoris

gracilis

gastrocnemius

peroneus longus

Almost all the muscles play a part in strenuous activity. Some muscles exert great force. Dozens of other muscles stay busy tensing or stabilizing different parts of the body and ensuring a safe posture and balance.

✋ TRY IT YOURSELF

Tense your upper arm as though trying to bend the elbow, but without movement. See and feel with your other hand how the main elbow-bending muscle, the *biceps brachii*, bulges with the strain.

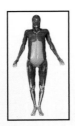

The shortest muscle fibers, only 0.04 of an inch in length, are in a tiny muscle called the stapedius, deep in each inner ear.

The sartorius leg muscle has the longest muscle fibers—about 12 inches long. This muscle crosses down the thigh from the hip to the inner knee.

Most muscles can also be passively stretched to more than twice their resting length, when their opposing, or antagonistic, muscle partner shortens.

MUSCLES *INSIDE A MUSCLE*

No matter a person's body shape—a thin, weak build, a bulky power-lifting champion, or a fit, strong athlete—all of his or her 640-plus muscles have the same inner structure and arrangement on the body and work in the same basic way.

Muscle Fibers

A single muscle is a collection of bundles of hair-thin fibers called myofibers. In cross-section, these bundles of myofibers resemble an electrical wire or optical fiber for a large communications cable. Muscle fibers range in size from 0.4 to 2 inches long and are thinner than cotton thread. A large muscle has several thousand fibers, arranged in groups of 100–200. Each group is wrapped in a strong covering and called a fascicle. The entire muscle is contained in a tough but flexible outer covering called the epimysium.

Muscle Fibrils

Each muscle fiber is only as thick as a human hair, yet it contains even thinner bundles called myofibrils. Within each myofibril, bundles of still tinier threadlike proteins (actin and myosin) slide past each other to shorten the myofibrils and fibers and contract the muscle.

HEALTH WATCH

A "twinge" from a muscle may warn that a strain or tear is likely. A strained, or "pulled," muscle occurs when some of the muscle fibers are damaged and torn. The muscle still works, but it swells, and movement is limited, tender, or painful. A ruptured muscle that has torn through so it cannot work at all is much more serious. This needs urgent medical attention.

TRY IT YOURSELF

Watch the inside of your wrist as you clench and loosen your fist. Notice the long tendons tightening under the skin. Tendons connect forearm muscles to bones in your hands so that you can curl your fingers.

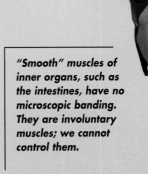

"Smooth" muscles of inner organs, such as the intestines, have no microscopic banding. They are involuntary muscles; we cannot control them.

Contraction

A typical muscle contracts mainly in its middle, or belly, region. The muscle's belly gets wider and bulges as the muscle shortens. Although the size of a contracted (flexed) muscle appears to change, its volume remains the same.

Muscle to Bone

Most muscles taper at each end into tough, ropelike fibers called tendons. Tendons are attached to the ends of a bone. As the muscle contracts, it pulls on the bone to produce movement. At the same time, other muscles help balance and stabilize the body without moving bones.

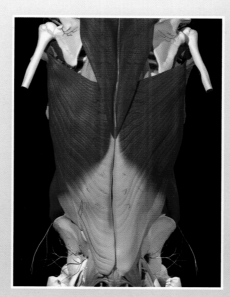

The "skeletal" muscles that we can control are called striated muscles. Under a microscope, these muscles display bands, or stripes, formed by the proteins actin and myosin.

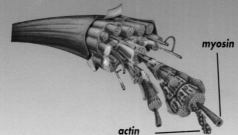

myosin

actin

IN FOCUS
Skeletal Muscles

A person pulling a truck hand over hand gradually works his way along the rope. The long, thin actin and thick myosin in muscles move past each other in a similar manner, making the muscle contract.

A thin layer of fat under the skin allows well-developed muscles to stand out more clearly. The deltoid is the muscle at the angle or point of the shoulder. From it, the triangular shaped pectoralis major slopes down to the lower center of the chest. The rectus abdominis muscle forms the "six-pack" on the front of the abdomen.

🗲 INSIDE A MUSCLE

A muscle is formed from a bundle of fibers, and each fiber is formed from a group of fibrils. A single fibril contains threads of proteins called myosin and actin. (See diagram.) Myosin and actin slide past each other to contract the muscle.

MUSCLES *In Control*

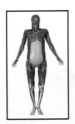

Our brains control our muscles. The brain sends out nerve signals that precisely direct each muscle to contract or relax. We have a total of more than 600 muscles, so the brain must send out hundreds of signals to all areas of the body every second.

Smooth and Skillful

Many movements happen almost automatically because we practice them many times. For example, the conscious thinking brain simply orders, "tie shoelaces." Then other parts of the brain, not involved in conscious thought, take care of the details. They fire off nerve signals to dozens of individual muscles in the arms, hands, and fingers to perform the complex and coordinated action of tying the laces. Muscles that we can control are called voluntary muscles.

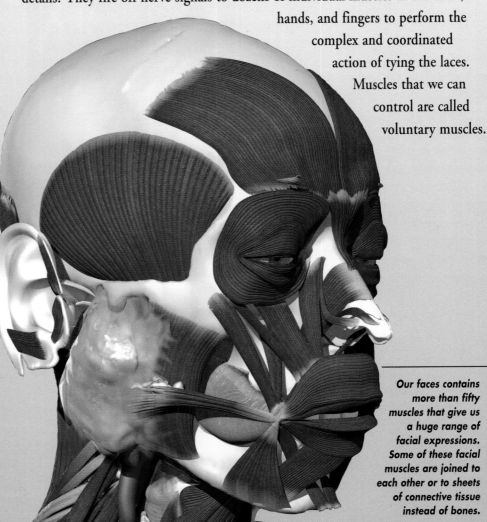

Our faces contains more than fifty muscles that give us a huge range of facial expressions. Some of these facial muscles are joined to each other or to sheets of connective tissue instead of bones.

Out of Control

We cannot consciously control all our muscles. Gut muscles and other internal organs work differently. Although the brain controls them, we cannot consciously make them do anything, no matter how strong our willpower or how hard we concentrate. These are called involuntary muscles.

Muscle Signals

A "motor" nerve (a nerve that sends signals to muscle fibers), along with the muscle fibers that it controls, is called a motor unit. Motor nerve endings branch to attach to individual muscle fibers. Some motor units control fewer than 10 muscle fibers. That means one nerve signal activates only those fibers, which permits very precise control such as in the tiny muscles that swivel the eyeball in its socket. The nerve in a motor unit for larger muscles, such as the thigh, may signal more than 1,000 muscle fibers to all contract at the same time.

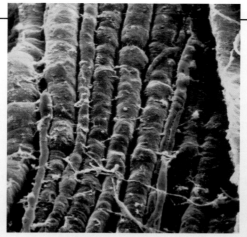

Extremely tiny muscle movements can greatly alter a facial expression. We communicate silently using these muscles. Often a slight smile or fleeting frown can "say" more than many words. Sometimes, our extreme expressions produce amusing, goofy faces!

IN FOCUS
Intricate Muscle Action

*When we walk, four front thigh muscles (the **quadriceps**—**rectus femoris** and three **vastus** muscles) pull our legs up and forward. The **biceps femoris**, part of our "hamstrings," runs down the backs of our thighs and stabilizes our knees.*
*The **gastrocnemius**, the calf muscle, extends our feet.*

*The leg is pulled backward at the hip by the **gluteus maximus** in the buttocks and by several muscles in the back of the thigh, including the **biceps femoris** and the **semitendinosus**, muscles that run down the backs of the thighs and attach below the knees.*

🐾 TRY IT YOURSELF

The *frontalis* muscle under the forehead lifts the eyebrows, and the *procerus* muscle at the bridge of the nose lowers and pulls them together. Look in a mirror while using these muscles. Try looking amazed (eyebrows highest), then annoyed (eyebrows lowest).

MUSCLES ON THE BRAIN

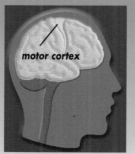

motor cortex

The brain's motor cortex (in yellow) controls movement by receiving and sending muscle nerve signals. Muscles that require very fine or precise control take up more space in the cortex. The brain stem (dark pink) controls automatic muscle movements, such as in the intestines.

The skeleton makes up from 40 to 50 percent of the body's total weight.

The average number of bones in a human skeleton is 206.

Our skeleton includes 28 skull bones, 26 vertebrae (backbones), 32 bones in each arm and hand, and 31 bones in each leg and foot.

About one in 20 people has two extra ribs—making 13 rib pairs instead of 12 pairs.

Three "floating" bones are embedded in muscle or tendons. The hyoid bone supports our tongue. Two patella (kneecaps) protect our knee joints.

BONES *Human Skyscraper*

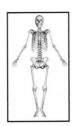

Old human bones in museums often appear white, rigid, flaky—and dead. Bones inside a living body are creamy gray, slightly flexible, smooth-surfaced—and very much alive.

Internal Skyscraper

Like the metal beams of a skyscraper, our bones form a strong inner framework that holds up our body's soft organs, nerves, and blood vessels. Our skeleton—all the bones together—give height, shape, solidity, and stability to our entire body.

Living Levers

Thanks to our skeleton and its ability to pull on muscles, our bodies have many examples of "living levers," especially in the arms and legs. For example, your biceps muscle acts like a lever when it moves your hand to touch your shoulder. Start with your arm straight out. Now bend your elbow. As your biceps muscle shortens (contracts), the elbow acts like the fulcrum of a lever. The upper end of our forearm bones (at the elbow) move only about an inch. This tiny movement causes the lower end of our forearm (our wrist) and our hand bones to move up to two feet with very little effort.

collarbone
(clavicle)

shoulder blade
(scapula)

humerus

breastbone
(sternum)

radius

ulna

wrist bones
(carpals)

finger bones
(phalanges)

fibula

shinbone
(tibia)

ankle bones
(tarsals)

Arms and legs share a similar bone arrangement. Both have one bone in their upper part, two bones in their lower part, a cluster of smaller bones in each wrist and ankle, and five sets of even smaller finger and toe bones in each hand and foot.

◉ HEALTH WATCH

Healthy bones need a regular supply of various minerals, especially calcium. This is very important for babies and children, whose bones are still growing. Calcium-rich foods include milk and other dairy products, eggs, green leafy vegetables, beans and peas, nuts, and shellfish.

— skull

jawbone (mandible)

Humans have an internal skeleton (endoskeleton) surrounded by muscles, organs, and other tissues. Animals such as crabs have an outer skeleton (exoskeleton) that forms a hard external case for the soft body tissues inside.

hipbone (pelvis)

thighbone (femur)

Able Protection

In addition to aiding in support and movement, the skeleton also protects our inner organs. The skull forms a strong, rigid case around the delicate brain. About seven bones on each side of the upper face form a bowl-shaped cavity, the orbit (eye socket), in which the eyeball nestles. The upper backbone, ribs, and breastbone create a flexible cage around the heart and lungs that not only shields these soft organs from physical damage, but also allows breathing movements.

🛡️ TWO-PART SKELETON

There are two main parts to the skeleton, the axial skeleton and the appendicular skeleton. The axial skeleton supports the body. It consists of 80 bones, including the skull, face bones, upper and lower jaws, spinal column, ribs, and breastbone. The appendicular includes the shoulders and hips. It contains a total of 126 bones that mostly "hang off" the axial skeleton. Our appendicular skeleton also forms our limbs—arms, wrists, hands, fingers, legs, ankles, feet, and toes.

● **Appendicular Skeleton**   ● **Axial Skeleton**

kneecap (patella)

foot bones (metatarsals)

toe bones (phalanges)

✋ TRY IT YOURSELF

Most bones are covered by layers of muscle and fat, connective tissue, and skin. In certain body areas, we can feel a bone just under thin skin. The point of the elbow is the end of the ulna, the main forearm bone. The lower ends of the lower leg bones—the tibia on the inside and fibula on the outside—form the hard lumps on either side of your ankles.

IN FOCUS
Muscles and Flexibility

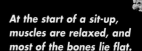

At the start of a sit-up, muscles are relaxed, and most of the bones lie flat.

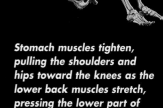

Stomach muscles tighten, pulling the shoulders and hips toward the knees as the lower back muscles stretch, pressing the lower part of the spine into the floor.

Hip joints pivot to swing the torso upright.

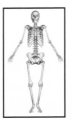

The longest bone in the body is the thighbone, or femur.

The largest and broadest bone is the ilium in the hip, or pelvis. Formed from six smaller bones firmly joined together, the pelvic "girdle" supports the soft abdominal organs and serves as an attachment for the legs.

The smallest bone is the stapes in the middle ear. It is hardly larger than this letter: U.

The strongest bone for its size is the lower jaw, called the mandible.

◉ HEALTH WATCH

Bones are tough—but sometimes not strong enough. High-speed impacts from a traffic accident, a sports injury, or a fall may cause breaks, or fractures. Do not move an injured person. Any movement can shift broken bones and damage softer body organs, such as nerves and blood vessels. Do not move someone who may have a back injury without special equipment to stabilize the spine. Always seek medical help for serious injuries, including fractures.

BONES *Bones Galore*

Bones provide an amazing example of strength combined with lightness. Each bone is exactly the right shape for attachment of muscles that withstand and produce powerful forces.

Shapes as Clues

Bones grow in many different shapes, and no two are exactly alike. For instance, the femurs in either thigh are similar, mirror images of each other but not identical. Several main shapes of bones give clues to their function.

Long and Short

Our main limb bones are long and slim to work like levers when we move our legs to walk or stretch our arms to reach something. The narrow main bone shaft saves weight while maintaining strength. Wide and knobby ends on the long bones provide a larger surface area where other muscles, ligaments, and tendons attach. Smaller, shorter bones fit together like puzzle pieces and are found mainly in the spinal column (backbone), wrists, and ankles. Groups of

The ribs form a cage around the delicate lungs and beating heart. Every rib is springy like tough plastic. Light pressure on the rib cage causes the bones to bend slightly rather than snapping and damaging the lungs.

Broken bones usually heal in a few months, provided they are "reduced," or put back into their original positions. Pins, screws, and thin metal strips may help bones knit together.

these smaller bones permit a limited range of flexibility. Flat bones, including the shoulder blades, hips, and breastbone, provide large surface areas for muscle attachments.

Inside a Bone

A typical long bone has three layers. On the outside is an extremely strong and dense "shell" of hard, or compact, bone. A honeycomblike inside layer called spongy, or cancellous, bone saves weight. Marrow, which looks like yellow or red jelly, fills the middle of the bone. Yellow bone marrow stores fat, while red bone marrow produces blood cells—especially red blood cells.

Activities that involve fast speeds or dangerous movements, such as mountain biking or skateboarding, require special safety precautions. Although the skull provides a strong natural casing for the brain, a helmet functions as a very helpful "second skull" around the body's most important organ.

Bones contain many minerals and nutrients—enough to feed an animal such as the leopard. Bone minerals include calcium, magnesium, phosphate, carbonate, and fluoride. The bone marrow uses iron to make blood cells. It can also store fat.

IN FOCUS
Bonehead

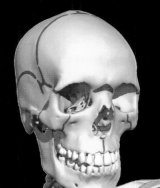

The upper dome (cranium) of the skull is formed from eight bones—the largest of which is the frontal bone of the forehead.

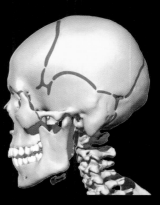

The parietal bone, near the upper side of the skull, fuses to the temporal bone below it. A hole in the lower middle of the temporal bone leads to the inner ear. Seven ringlike cervical vertebrae (neck bones) support the skull.

 TRY IT YOURSELF

Human bodies vary in proportions, especially in the lengths of arms, legs, and main body, or torso. The femur accounts for about one-quarter of an adult's height, but this proportion is lower in a younger person who is still growing. Foot length is typically one-sixth of overall height. How do you measure up?

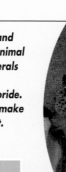

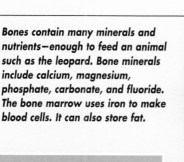

MICROSCOPIC BONE TISSUE

Bones seem solid but contain thousands of "tunnels," called haversian canals, for nerves and blood vessels. Many layers of hard bone matrix encircle the canals like the rings of a tree. The dark, spidery-looking shapes are bone-making cells, or osteocytes. Each unit is called a haversian system, or osteon.

BONES *BUSY BONES*

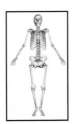

Bones not only support, move, and protect the body, but also produce blood cells, provide storage for minerals and fat, and adapt to stresses and strains by slightly remodeling their shape.

Wet Bones

Water accounts for about one-fifth of the weight of every bone. The bones of a healthy adult contain more than a half gallon of water. Bones of a skeleton become very brittle and lighter as the water inside slowly evaporates.

Thirsty Work

A rich supply of nerves and blood vessels weaves through small canals from the hard outer bone layers to the spongy inner bone and marrow areas to control and nourish this vital connective tissue with important fluids and minerals. Blood flowing back to the body from the bone marrow carries new blood cells to replace the cells that wear out and die as part of natural body maintenance. The new blood cells include oxygen-carrying red blood cells and disease-fighting white blood cells that are produced by the skeleton at the rate of three million every second!

HEALTH WATCH

Calcium is an important mineral that aids muscle contraction. When a person's diet is low in calcium, however, the body "borrows" it from bones, making them weaker and more prone to injury. Osteoporosis—loss of bone mass—is an age-related disease caused when bone tissue is broken down faster than new bone tissue is produced. Bones become thinner and weaker. Osteoporosis usually affects older people, especially women. People who exercise regularly throughout life strengthen their bones, which may help prevent the disease.

TRY IT YOURSELF

Bone bends less than cartilage. Place your thumb on the end of your nose (cartilage) and wiggle it. Then try the same movement on the bridge of your nose (bone).

Our feet are complicated structures with many inner pieces. Each foot contains 26 bones of varying shapes and sizes. Intricate sets of muscles, nerves, arteries, and veins weave through the ankles, feet, and toes.

A Big Break

Nerves, like blood vessels, wind throughout bone tissue. Some of these nerves tell us whether a bone is bending too much or aches from infection. Broken bones cause very sharp and severe pain. Bones are also dynamic. They react to stress—such as exercise—by growing thicker and denser. Through a process called remodeling, a bone can slightly reshape itself to deal with any extra demands placed upon it. The change in shape helps the entire skeleton deal with most increases in physical activities. Bones that are not kept active become weak and brittle. When inactive bones are suddenly put under extra stress, they snap!

IN FOCUS
Nervous Bones

Space's weightless, or zero-G (no-gravity), state puts very little strain or pressure on someone's bones. Astronauts must exercise daily while in space to keep their bones and muscles strong and healthy.

Even in our gravity-controlled environment here on the Earth, it is just as important to exercise regularly in order to keep bones in the best possible condition. This will help to prevent gradual weakening over time.

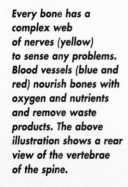

Every bone has a complex web of nerves (yellow) to sense any problems. Blood vessels (blue and red) nourish bones with oxygen and nutrients and remove waste products. The above illustration shows a rear view of the vertebrae of the spine.

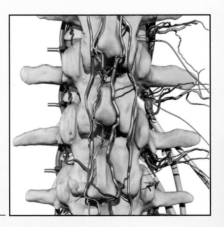

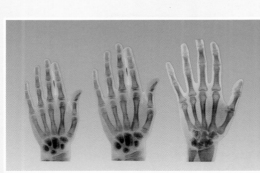

OSSIFICATION

As bones develop from infancy to adulthood, they gradually become harder and stronger. Bones form first as cartilage (a tough, elastic tissue). Cartilage hardens at different rates and changes into true bone in a process called ossification. For example, wrist bones do not fully ossify until the teenage years.

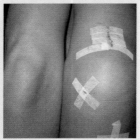
The largest single joint in the body is the knee. Two knuckle-shaped ends on the lower end of the femur fit into shallow depressions in the top of the tibia.

As the knee straightens, the bones twist slightly to "lock" the joint and make the leg rigid from hip to ankle.

The knee's "floating bone," the patella, (kneecap) protects the front of this essential leg joint.

BONES *Twists and Turns*

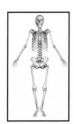

A joint is where two bones meet. Joints allow the body to bend and twist in many different directions. Your body has hundreds of joints. Without them, your skeleton would be so rigid you wouldn't be able to move at all.

Inside a Joint

Most joints allow movement. Inside a joint, tendons attach muscles to bones, and ligaments join bones to bones. A synovial membrane forms a baglike covering, or synovial capsule, that encases a joint. The membrane produces a slippery liquid called synovial fluid that, like the oil in a car engine, lubricates a joint to reduce friction, wear, and tear. The joint capsule forms a tougher "bag" surrounding the synovial capsule and helps keep the bones in the joint together.

Joint Design

Joints allow different types and ranges of movement. The hinge joint of the knee allows the lower leg to swing forward and backward, but not far to either side. Vertebral joints between each backbone are cushioned by flexible pads called intervertebral disks. Each bone tilts slightly, but the series of spinal joints allows us to bend our backs almost in half.

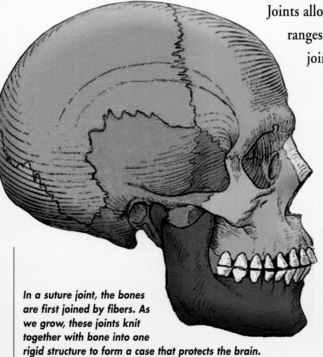

In a suture joint, the bones are first joined by fibers. As we grow, these joints knit together with bone into one rigid structure to form a case that protects the brain. Faint squiggly lines remain visible where the ends of the skull bones sutured themselves together.

A joint flexed (bent) too far causes discomfort or pain. Regular exercise and proper stretching techniques gradually increase flexibility of joints. High levels of flexibility allow an effortless, natural range of movement without discomfort.

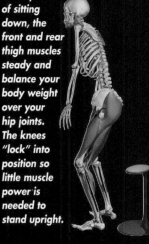

In the process of sitting down, the front and rear thigh muscles steady and balance your body weight over your hip joints. The knees "lock" into position so little muscle power is needed to stand upright.

🖐 TRY IT YOURSELF

The shoulder and hip are both ball-and-socket joints. The shallow shoulder socket allows the ball-shaped upper end of the humerus a wide range of movement. You can rotate your arm in nearly a full circle. The deeper hip socket limits your leg movement.

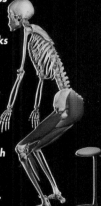

The **gluteus maximus** muscles in the buttocks pull hard to swing the femur down and back at the hip joint. The lower thigh muscles bend the knee joint.

Human body joints cannot compare with those of a spider monkey's amount of flexibility. Our leg joints are designed for weight bearing, which limits the range of movement. Monkeys use all four limbs as they move around, so their arms and legs look very similar.

INSIDE THE KNEE

Shiny cartilage covers the knuckle-like lower ends of the femur shown in this rear view of the leg. The ligaments (white cords) around and within the knee are stretchy, or elastic, to prevent overextension. A bone that slips out of its normal position is dislocated and must be maneuvered back into place.

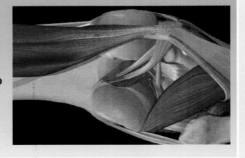

Sitting down mainly involves the hips and knees. Spine and hip bones stay upright. The top of the femur swivels in its ball-and-socket joint to form a right angle with the hipbone.

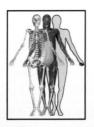

ALL TOGETHER *Full Steam Ahead*

In a running race against the animal kingdom, even a person who holds a world speed record would most likely lose. If the contest were broadened to several events, from a sprint to a marathon to a long swim, then the human body's all-around training and athletic abilities might begin to win.

Maximum human running speeds decrease as distance increases. The fastest speed record for the 100-meter dash is 9.58 seconds, or 23 miles per hour (mph). The fastest time for a marathon (26.2 miles) is just over two hours.

Performance levels peak when the heart reaches its maximum constant pumping rate. The lungs also have a maximum rate at which they can absorb the needed levels of oxygen.

Hard-working muscles produce waste products, such as lactic acid.

In water, fish are fastest, reaching speeds of more than 67 mph. Human swimmers can achieve speeds of about 4.5 mph in sprint swims, mostly thanks to powerful arm strokes.

Arms and Legs

We humans enjoy a variety of movements because our arms are different from our legs. Most other land animals have four similar limbs designed for weight bearing, walking, running, and jumping. Our legs carry our weight and move us from place to place, freeing our arms to a wider range of movements, such as balancing the body on a narrow beam or hanging

HEALTH WATCH

Sudden, severe movement stresses the body's muscles, joints, and bones and easily causes sprains and strains. Athletes should warm up for best results. They may stretch, jog, or do similar light exercises to help the muscles adjust and to get their joints moving freely. After the workout or competition, they "cool down" with more stretching and other light movements to ease the muscles and joints back into normal patterns of activity.

HUMAN The fastest human sprinters reach a speed of nearly 25 miles per hour, but only for a short distance. Arm movements assist the legs by pumping like pendulums—giving added momentum to each stride. After about half a mile, the speed falls to roughly 16 mph.

RHINO The fastest animal sprinter among large mammals is the rhinoceros. At a weight of two tons or more, it can pound along at peak speeds of more than 29 mph. A human can never expect to outpace a charging rhino.

from a rope or bar. Also, most animals instinctively swim if they fall into or willingly enter water. Although humans must learn to swim, they have devised several different swimming strokes powered mainly by the arms.

Brain and Body

Muscles, bones, and joints work as an amazingly complex and coordinated system. Even in simple movements, such as walking or eating, hundreds of muscles pull on bones and flex or stabilize joints. We must also recognize the important role the brain plays in our wide-ranging capacity for different movements. Our large brain allows us to learn, practice, and refine new movements. As athletes know, humans use intelligence and concentration to gradually make movements more effective and efficient. Animals learn new movements in a much simpler way, and often only as a matter of survival. In ten Olympic events between humans and animals, who do you think might win?

🖐 TRY IT YOURSELF

The world record for the long jump is almost 30 feet. Measure this length outdoors or in a large room. The high jump record is nearly 8 feet. Measure this height distance as well, but be aware that many ceilings, especially in homes, are also 8 feet high! These records show the incredible feats set by the fittest, best-trained human bodies. Try the long jump yourself. How far can you jump? Do not try the high jump without special safety equipment.

OSTRICH The fastest (and heaviest) bird runs on two legs, like a human, which makes its speed more comparable to ours. Ostriches can race at almost 45 mph for short distances and can maintain speeds up to 22.5 mph for a few miles.

CHEETAH The cheetah's long limbs, powerful muscles, and flexible back, which arches up and down to increase stride length, make it a running machine—and the fastest of all animals. These large cats can burst into speeds approaching 70 mph. After half a minute, however, these sleek African sprinters are nearly exhausted.

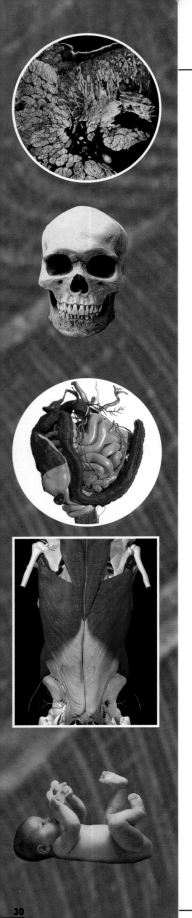

G l o s s a r y

actin the thinner of the two threadlike strands of main muscle-cell proteins in myofibrils that slide between similar threads of myosin as a muscle contracts.

atrophy the wasting and weakening of a muscle or body part from disuse.

calcium an important dietary mineral that gives hardness and strength to bones and teeth.

cancellous bone the honeycombed, spongy-looking bone tissue found in the middle layer of most bones that helps give bones their strength.

cartilage a strong, smooth, shiny, and slightly flexible substance, sometimes called "gristle," that forms body parts, such as the nose and ears, and protects and cushions the ends of bones in joints.

cells the billions of tiny building blocks of the body that form the different body organs and tissues.

collagen a tough, fibrous type of connective tissue protein that gives skin and tendons strength and elasticity.

compact bone the hard, dense, very strong bone tissue that forms the outer layer, or "shell," of most bones.

cranium the domed upper part of the skull that covers the brain.

dermis the inner, or lower, layer of skin tissue under the epidermis that contains blood vessels, hair roots, and touch sensors (nerve endings).

elastin a strong, flexible microfiber that allows blood vessels, skin, and other organs, such as the stomach and intestines, to bend and stretch.

epidermis the outermost, surface layer of skin that is mostly dead and is continually being worn away.

follicle a tiny pit or "pocket" in the skin from which a hair grows.

genes the chemical code inside cells that determines how organisms form.

integumentary system the skin.

keratin the hard, strong, tough tissue that forms hair and nails and is found in the outer layer (epidermis) of skin.

lactic acid a by-product of muscle activity that is usually carried away by the blood. Lactic acid buildup causes fatigue, soreness, or cramps.

ligament a strong, slightly stretchy fibrous tissue that holds together bones at a joint, allowing a certain extent of movement.

marrow the soft, jellylike substance inside some bones that may store fat or produce new blood cells.

muscle organized groups of fibers that attach to bone or each other and contract to produce movement.

myofibers thin, threadlike strands of tissue that form bundles inside a muscle. Each myofiber consists of even finer strands of myofibrils.

myofibrils extemely fine, threadlike strands of actin and myosin that form bundles inside a myofiber.

myosin the thicker of the two threadlike strands of main muscle-cell proteins in myofibrils that slide between similar threads of actin as a muscle contracts.

ossification the gradual hardening of tissue, such as cartilage, into bone.

osteon (haversian system) a bone-tissue unit that grows like layers of tree rings surrounding a haversian canal and includes living bone cells, called osteocytes, as well as ossified bone.

perspiration the watery, salty liquid produced by sweat glands. As sweat evaporates, it cools the body.

sebaceous glands tiny skin glands next to every hair that produce natural oils and waxes to lubricate the skin and keep it water-repellent.

skeleton the set of bones that forms the framework of the body, supports the muscles, and protects internal organs.

smooth muscle (also called unstriated muscle or involuntary muscle) muscle that we cannot control, such as that found in bladder walls, stomach, and intestines.

striped muscle (also called striated muscle, skeletal muscle, or voluntary muscle) muscle that we can control, such as that found in our arms, legs, hands, feet, and throughout our faces.

suture a nonmobile bone junction of the adult skull, usually visible as a faint squiggly line, that forms when the separate skull bones knit together at maturity.

synovial fluid a thick, slippery liquid inside most joints that works like lubricating oil to make movements smoother and reduce joint wear.

tendon a strong, ropelike fibrous tissue that connects a muscle to a bone or a muscle to another muscle.

vertebra one of the individual bones that makes up the spinal column.

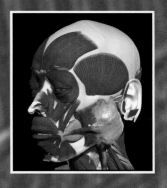

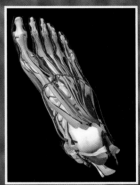

METRIC CONVERSION TABLE

AREA
1 square yard = 0.8 square meter

1 square inch = 6.5 square centimeters

WEIGHT
1 pound = 0.45 kilogram

LENGTH
1 inch = 2.54 centimeters

VOLUME
1 cup = 0.24 liter

1 gallon = 3.8 liters

SPEED
1 mile per hour = 1.6 kilometers per hour

25 miles per hour = 40 kilometers per hour

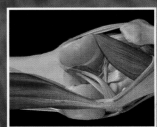

I n d e x

North American edition copyright © TickTock Entertainment Ltd. 2010.
First published in North America in 2010 by New Forest Press, PO Box 784, Mankato, MN 56002
www.newforestpress.com
ISBN: 978-1-84898-330-4 Library of Congress Control Number: 2010925191 Tracking number: nfp0005 Printed in the USA
We would like to thank Elizabeth Wiggans, Jenni Rainford, and Dr. Kristina Routh for their help with this book.

Picture credits: t (top), b (bottom), c (center), l (left), r (right)
Alamy: Cover (left), 5tl, 9tc, 9c, 9bc, 12tl, 13c, 14-15c, 15c, 18tl, 19tc, 19cr, 20bc, 21tc, 22-23c, 24bc, 25c, 25tr, 25ct, 26bc, 27tl,
28b. Mediscan:12-13c, 13t. Primal Pictures: Cover (right), 7tr, 9tr, 11tr, 13tr, 15tr, 17tr, 19tr, 20-21c, 21tr, 21cr, 23tr, 27tr, 29tr,
29cr. Science Photo Library: 4 (all), 9br, 11c, 13cr, 15bc, 17tc, 19c, 23cr, 26tl, 27tc, 27b, 29-30c, 29br, 30tl. Shutterstock: 6b, 21t.